# POEMS AND MELODRAMAS

# DONALD DAVIE

# Poems and Melodramas

CARCANET

First published in 1996 by
Carcanet Press Limited
402-406 Corn Exchange Buildings
Manchester M4 3BY

A CIP catalogue record for this book
is available from the British Library
ISBN 1 85754 290 8

The publisher acknowledges financial assistance
from the Arts Council of England

Set in 10pt Palatino by Bryan Williamson, Frome
Printed and bound in England by SRP Ltd, Exeter

## Acknowledgements

'Women and War' was written at the time of *To Scorch or Freeze*, but no written record of it survives. The version printed here was transcribed from a tape recording.

The typescripts of 'Fatherhood' and 'Reticence' were found in a book by Donald Davie in the possession of Professor Bernard Bergonzi.

'Tiger at the Movie-Show' was first published in *Prospect*, summer 1949; 'Immortal Longings. Before Surgery' in *Thames Poetry*, winter 1976; 'The Bent' in *The American Scholar*, autumn 1980; 'Bearing Witness' in the *Cambridge Review*, June 1987; 'Two Intercepted Letters' in *Sequoia*, Centennial Issue 1987; 'On Edmund Spenser's House in Ireland' in *Cumberland Poetry Review*, Fall 1988; 'Our Father' in *The Tyndale Society Journal*, June 1995, and (in full) in *PN Review* 107. To the editors of these publications acknowledgement is due.

The other poems included in *Poems and Melodramas* were written after *To Scorch or Freeze*. The *Melodramas* are for the most part from the same period and *PN Review* published some of them.

# Contents

*Poems*

*Seven Melodramas*

## Bits and Pieces

Harmonious first and last,
a classical composure,
is what the republican mentors
ask of a verse in your honour.

For them to accredit it,
bits here and pieces there
knocked together aren't
sufficiently severe.

And no doubt they are right.
Clear-eyed accommodations
don't measure up to our sessions;
neither do porticos.

Composites, inspired
improvisations on
the one part and the other,
make up the script of our love.

Ah my Isotta, I'd
raise you a temple not
less ramshackle than
the one in Rimini.

## The Knave of Hearts

*for Vikram Seth*

The accomplished *hetaira* toys for this Knave of Hearts.
Though he writes his poems as often in English as Urdu,
He speaks for a culture where the courtesan
Is the honoured exponent of more than one of the arts.

Imagine a bimbo as conversant with
Fanshawe and Waller as with Tennyson!
She would attract a different clientèle,
Not more in love with her than with Purcell.

Seductive magic of the Knave of Hearts,
Lovely and winning, but impossible . . .
He cannot trump the Ace of deadly Spades:
A rule in our game and in his as well.

## The Lost Bride

### *(Arkhangelsk, 1943)*

'Versify it, Donald,'
I hear one of them say;
'Put it in rhyme, if I'm
To give it the time of day!'

And level-headed you
See the force of that:
'Unable to join the dance,
Keep still and sit it out.'

Dear vanished one, alive
As I have to imagine, your
Booted foot beats out: 'Not
Up to it any more.'

It is the dancer's verdict
On the irredeemable clown,
His feet all asplay, although with
A clumsiness all his own.

Younger grizzled men
In Spain and Morbihan
At this very hour take drams
To greet the unwelcome dawn.

Hours later, the concerned
Seeking a fuddled answer
Get only this: 'In youth
I loved a dancer.'

## Orvieto. *The King of Clubs*

If I should riffle a pack
Of playing-cards in sight
Of the Duomo's façade
(Angular Gothic, three-gabled),
It should be the King of Clubs
Turns up, and answers back.

Nowhere except in untrue
Photographs is it a wall,
Not even a screen. From whatever
Angle you look at it close,
It is all of a ripple, three
Dimensions, nowhere two.

And this you take for *richesse*.
But it is more disconcerting:
There are in the end no walls,
Nothing to screen us. Whatever
We took to be safely outward
Implicates us no less.

Once he was King of the rustics,
His clubs were staves. Now trefoil,
Three knobs on a whistling stalk,
They smite us out of the blue as
In an archaic, armoured
Affray of singlesticks.

Sidelong or in wristy backlash
This Gothic emperor bruises.
Come close; in his gilt, his marbled
In-and-out, there is no
Place to escape his buffets.
You owe, though you paid in cash.

Serpentine is the edge
And hazard of it. That
Enemy, the serpent,
Has our measure, as
Card-players in the gardens
Of the *fortezza* acknowledge.

Clubs take the rubbers, mostly.
Drubbed, the King of Hearts
Meekly, modestly sweeps
The board under his coat as
Night comes in. The game
He covertly wins is ghostly.

## On the Final Day

*for Charles Tomlinson, concerning Ivor Gurney*

No, there will be no explanations then:
Not mine of myself to God (who knows me through)
Nor God's of Himself to me concerning (say)
Ivor Gurney. He will not explain;
Illuminate sometimes, but not explain.

You'd have 'illuminate' equal to 'enlighten'.
The etymology bears you out, but not
The history of those two English words.
The land, the language – they are not the same;
And Eden isn't either one's right name.

Eden is what we forfeited, once for all:
His first illumination, ground of the rest.
Read, for 'Gloucester', England; read, for 'English',
Catalan, Hebrew, Navajo. Which is best?
Too plain our answer spells self-interest.

Foredoomed, poor flailing Gurney! Mostly we
Aren't, but seek out a doom not meant for us.
The muddy flash – our brief flame soon eclipsed –
Flares out, reveals it. His, in the madhouse, flames
To glorify God, and all our exploits tames.

See Charles Tomlinson, *Jubilation* (1995), p.60

*To C.T.*

We have shown each other the tricks
Of an abstruse trade
For fifty years, old friend;
Now to an attentive
Third party, did such exist,
An array of certain tics
In the deployment of words
Would amount to a common style,
Disconcertingly similar
From your hand and from mine.

Will he even notice,
This improbable person,
That at your hand and mine
The style serves a different end?

Hearing the same promise
Made on behalf of a godchild,
Will he notice our gods
Cannot be reconciled?

See Charles Tomlinson, *Annunciations* (1989), p.55

## Thomas and Emma

Not deaf to ghosts yet not expecting them
I paced the hill-rim's shadowy belvedere
At Shaftesbury, when from the abbey ruins
An old thin voice pronounced, for me to hear:

'A levelled, levelling culture leaves no room
For amorous or other compliment.
Analogy and allusion are ruled out;
Our happiness can have no monument.'

A voice returned: 'The happiness alleged
To have obtained between us never was,
Or else so seldom that a truthful culture
Rightly discounts hyperboles like yours.'

In the event I heard both voices falter.
Hyperbole, analogy, allusion
Build up what is no lie, although so wishful:
Conspiratorial, conjugal collusion.

This, though unsettled, was a summer's day –
I took another turn along the grass
And gravel of the rampart. Overhead
The boughs soughed something. It was not: 'Alas.'

## To a Staffordshireman, from a Devon Villa

I went to war once, I'm not sure for what
But not for Eden. I'd no thought of that,
Religious or irreligious. I was glad
To go, for what till then I'd never had,
The heedlessness of youth. From Staffordshire,
Yorkshire and Gloucester, Devon, for the mere
Adventure of it 'in a righteous cause',
The unlicked levies came to earn applause.
The blamelessness of that, the poignancy,
Has never ceased, and will not cease, to move me;
But Eden, Avon? Come, we knew the date,
Raw though we were; we knew it was too late
For moonlit meadow umbels. War kept sane
Gurney, whose chromosomes played him up again
Only when peace came. Do I have to say
That war, however garlanded with may
And Tewkesbury towers, prefigures our perdition?
Its therapy, though, can manage a remission
In a woe that, once the armistice lets it loose,
Drives the sufferer out of civic use.

Such harsh sentiments are bold and loud;
Nothing umbrageous niceties can't cloud
With a good conscience. But, clipped or ornate,
Horatian diction cannot mitigate
Horrors reserved to crown a later date.
Horace was shrewd, but knew of nothing fit
For Edward Thomas's death or the manner of it.
My door swings open for you always, but
In another's mouth 'Sabine' might keep it shut.

See Charles Tomlinson, *Jubilation* (1995), pp.43-44

## Jottings, not so Random

1

'He's a sad sack. So's he.'
Does the 'sad' a little
Mitigate the 'sack'?
No; I meant to belittle.


2

Infinite Wisdom and Pure Mind
Are not even distant cousins;
The one advises prudence,
The other cozens.


3

One thing you can say
For the Devil Incarnate:
The embodiment means you can
Rub him the wrong way.


4

Pure Mind and Satan are,
Paul Valéry observes,
Near kin. Can Theory say
Which serves, and which subserves?


5

Pure Mind. Never mind that it is
Demonstrably impure;
It keeps its promises,
Like Mephistopheles.

6

Though what we've a mind to is
For the most part muddle,
Most lethal among our toys
Is not that, but ill-will.


7

Rubbing the wrong way
Is an allowable mischief,
I judge: it is undertaken
To nettle, not belittle.

## Sea of Tiberias

'Prevalent, his death he pleads.'

The man on the foreshore cooking a fish breakfast
Was a King Arthur or a Deadwood Dick,
Not false and yet not actual; between
The Resurrection and the Ascension, Christ
Had turned into (what couldn't be right) a legend.

The man on the foreshore might have seen the shoal
Break surface in an unregarded quarter.
By trawlers of a sterile night he might
(Given the dawn's eleventh-hour draught of fishes)
Be credited with legendary know-how.

Revenants are not unheard of, nor
Are the uncanny masters of a trade;
Every locality has wind of them.
But what was designed for Him was such a transfer
As makes the hairs at the back of my neck stand up.

The ghost that was a revenant departed
Along with its localities. Succeeded
A sort of Ghost that would be known as Holy:
Prevalent, but not as Error is;
Prevailing for us sufferers everywhere.

## Seeing through Me

'The dead shall look me thro' and thro''
(*In Memoriam*)

'Mesmerized eyes on one's
Dead fathers, not on one's
Unborn sons': a verdict
Stage-managed to convict
This line of Tennyson's.

It happened no longer ago
Than 1969;
'A foul proposition', opine
The worthies of that era.
So little did they know.

Now men choose to be sterile,
They do not know their sons
No, nor their daughters, each
A threat to a life-style out of
Fortunate Tennyson's reach.

'The dead shall know me through
And through.' Not shall, but do.
Is it Mesmer's, is it Freud's
Client most lightly avoid what
Eternity amounts to?

The forebears, whose defaced
Gravestones endure the tread
Of sceptical visitors,
Are vindicated, seeing
They see though they are dead.

See John Fowles, *The French Lieutenant's Woman* (1969), chapter 48

## Toby to Aguecheek

My mountain belly and incontinent girth
That strutted, more than trod, the groaning earth

Have, in some questionings of saluted merit
Worried that sheer bulk balks the encroaching spirit.

Carnality. But we worship the Incarnate:
Buried in the ageing flesh, or blossoming in it?

I who cull those blossoms know the truth:
Gross age engrosses all we risked in youth.

A fat man is as like to be a saint
As any hermit skeletal in paint,

I tell myself, and with more confidence
Now, in advanced age, needing her carnal presence

Whom no, my lean fastidious friend, you have
Not so much as entertained a thought of.

## War Criminal

He had the gift of being pitiless;
Rare he thought it, though in that he was wrong.
It was his only talent, and I picked
Away at it I cannot say how long.

Bride to one past saving, him I bridled;
And he (poor dear) came bit by bit to function
Shorn of the one citation that he cherished,
The serving soldier's: 'Served without compunction'.

Vengeance is mine, mine only, saith the Lord;
That is to say, past our capacities.
We do, however, wreak as it we can,
And that is allowed, but do not call it Justice.

## Ecclesiastical Polity

*(The Laws of . . .* by Richard Hooker, 1597)

'Not what's done, but what
Is done religiously . . .'
Hooker proposed. Accounts
That credit him with Laws
Of Pusillanimity
Pretend that this amounts to:
'It is the thought that counts.'

His long book of short views
(Short as he was with profaneness),
Because he was deferential
To long-established use
Has made him seem to profess
'Nothing succeeds like success',
That sorriest of long views.

The *via media*, that
Anglican offer to trimmers,
Was not his style of play.
Marrying Rome with Geneva
Would always tax the Believer
Sorely, he thought; no grimace
Nor smirk would blow it away.

Unread, he is still co-opted
To shore up the C. of E.,
Though long ago that adopted
Expediently a more
Beguiling polity
That keeps abreast of the times.
(What else are Synods for?)

Against the rigorist Cartwright
Hooker was in the right.
But now, since he sought to construe
The Laws in a liberal light,
He is thought to set Law on its head;
So little is a true
Liberality admitted.

## Women and War

Rebuke the company of spearmen
Trampling in wedges of silver.
Scatter the peoples that delight in war,
The Seventh Fleet and the Sixth.

They are not in pains as other men
And they are not gorged as other men,
Therefore the pride wind about them as a chain.
The apparel of violence hath covered them so that
　　　　　　　　they feel little.

Their eyes pop. Affluent princes,
They have overpassed the thoughts of their heart,
They swim afloat and talk, they speak from aloft
Saying 'sanctuaries', they have no thought of Zion.

But the Lord shall give matter of talk
To the concourse of women reporters.
Miriam and her sisters who sang the praise upon timbrels,
Daughters of the Confederacy and of recaptured Zion,
　　　　　　　　and of the Primrose League,
Distributors of white feathers.

He maketh men to be of one mind in an house.
He shall have pity upon the poor
And shall save the lives of the poor,
And precious shall their blood be in his sight.

## 'Our Father'

### I. *On a hint from Bertolucci*

Passed from you, mother, to the custody
Of another, and that other, though a Muse,
Acerbic, limited, can I think I am
Worth your nine months' indignity and labour?
The Muse you may have vowed me to was not
The one I find I'm serving. In the clear
Service of dream you come to me, forgiving
Although unsmiling:
                          'Look, your father's here.'


### II *On another*

> *'venne il padre'*

He is the delineator, here he comes,
Diffident porter of the primal hues
To the palette of his endowed but ailing
Child, the devoted homemaker who scumbles
To glories of old rose, of Cambridge blue,
Of less than Irish green to pin the wilting
And waxing indeterminacies of verdure.

Comes the Father, the delineator,
Master of line and of the primary,
Behind the scenes the guarantor of Nature,
Not the all-round factotum that he seems.


### III *Green*

Issue of yellow's intercourse with blue,
Green is no primary hue. Though every Spring
Persuade us of its primacy, it is not
The unmediated progeny of the Father.

18

'Father, saddest of all my brethren, father.'
Franco Fortini, what were you thinking of?
Brothers have all one father. Are there no
Odds between filial and fraternal love?

Lincoln green, fraternity of the greenwood...
But blue or yellow is His blazon, he
Sired King John no less than Robin Hood.
Being the Father, he is no man's fellow.


IV   *Alfieri*

Tragedian of an Italy then unborn,
He cudgelled himself for having prostituted
The buskin to the tiara; that's to say,
His play to the scrutiny of the Holy Father.

Later he learned how much more tolerant an
Unpolished pontiff was, than a godless State
That asked a theatre for Everyman,
The man first dulled, then frivolously diverted.

Later again (we look beyond him now)
The buskin throve by dirtying – the tiara
And then the Cross; which lives by seeing how
Unwearyingly the Father's sons revile him.


V   *To a Neophyte*

Do not fancy that the 'oh' and 'ah'
Which may escape me signify the cut
And smoothing face of the Father's chisel are
Soon or blithely suffered. They are not.

From me, although acerb, no epigrams.
Much as I'm enamoured of the terse,
Frauds self-confessed, self-interested scams...
Shameful, the in-house dailiness of verse!

19

The mother of all battles, and the father
Of every cock-up . . . that's an issue reckoned
By a superior calculus. Would you rather
Side with the first, or sign up with the second?

Whichever daunting parent gets your voice,
Recollect:
                 To start with, you'd no choice.


VI   *After Whittier*

    ('Dear Lord and Father of Mankind')

Carnival-master, Father, god of the glitch,
Functionary of the out-of-phase,
Apparent fumbler tripping the wrong switch,
Dear gremlin Lord, frustrate our foolish ways.


VII   *After Watts*

Behold! what wondrous grace
    The Father has bestow'd
On sinners of a mortal race –
    To call them sons of God!

We would no longer lie
    Like slaves beneath the throne;
My faith shall *Abba* Father, cry,
    And Thou the kindred own.

It does not yet appear
    How great we must be made;
But when we see our Saviour here,
    We shall be like our head.

VIII   *Good Friday*

'God the Son is our brother.'
Not true, but let it pass;
It's not for a splendid sibling
Good Friday cries, 'Alas!'

For also it cries, 'All hail!'
'Papa!' it cries, and is
Thereupon desolate
Past help of therapies.

Not how we are begotten,
That prurient 'primal scene',
But how it is to be fathered
Is what our tremblings mean.


IX   'That he should be so severe'

That he should be so severe
In what He asks of us
(For so it seems) – is this
Love, so onerous?

True, it springs of an action
Beyond engendering;
But it is felt as some
Less amiable thing.

On our idea of 'father'
Fed, if we're lucky, by
Memories of indulgence
(Kicking a ball in the alley),

Ancient Israel leaves
Its inexpungible mark:
A Father no less father
For being patriarch.

A patriarch prone to cock-ups
Is not what we would choose;
But we have no choice in the matter
Any more than the Jews.

And would it be fun in the alley,
Trying to out-shoot
A preternatural marksman,
Dad's infallible boot?

Omnipotent, oh yes;
Not omni-talented.
See Him walk back to his mark,
Shaking a worried head.

What can it be but love
That He is tendering,
Possessed of so much power
So much surrendering?

## On Edmund Spenser's House in Ireland

Every so often, Lord, the wanton muse
– So, or in some such strain, the mantled stump
Kilcolman semaphored unwelcome news
Across a mile of bog and Munster damp,
Harrier-haunted. . . . Not as we would choose
(For we would go, Lord, where you set your stamp)
But every so often still, the unruly muse
Yearns for the flowery noon, the midnight lamp.
Elysiums out of nowhere: compositions!
The workaday exigencies of prose
Serve best, in us and Spenser, the tame missions
You seem to have assigned us. Only those
Who famously once were prey to faerie visions
Flag home to you. Ourselves we must compose.

# Two Intercepted Letters

*in memoriam* Philip Larkin,
*ob.* 2 December 1985.

1

'Southey! Alas, my writings
Are not on slate: no finger,
Not Time's that is
Dipped in the clouds of years,
In freezing rains that split
The monumental stone,
Rubs out the written. Byron
I had avoided, slighted; he
(Byron) knew it; he did not
Love Landor; he could not.

Injurious print
Outlasts all slate, although
What's said should be unsaid
Of Byron dead.'

2

'A ghoulish, ghoulish, ghastly business this,
Mr Nollekens! No one when I
Was 'prenticed mason, rustic archivist,
Told me the verb I'd conjugate was "die".

Epitaphs are very well. But, sir,
Tell me by what wise exercise of will
The elegist in need of custom jibs
Short of where "die" shades over into "kill".

Here in Northampton I have traffic with
Lord Byron and such spectres. I declare
Grave-robbers, monsters, had recruited me.
From that morne service spare, I plead, John Clare.'

## Bearing Witness

Bearing and giving are different, it appears.

In the latter case (constrained)
one supposes, or may suppose,
a judge and a jury. In the case of

bearing

witness, there is a load
that has to be discharged
in physical fact, the weight
on the grieving shoulders
thankfully hefted off,
a sack into the shadows of God's barton.

No judge, no jury, but one,
that one incalculable, His
authority established by no statute.

No one expects a verdict. Man
bears like a weight in the gut
witness, a load that
must be evacuated
in the hedge-bottom or elsewhere.

Thus it is with the witness
of poetry, for instance.

## The Bent

Thinking how it is
   too late to undertake
      one more dutiful office
against my bent ('the grain',
   I called it once), too late
      to make as much as can
be made of Zukofsky's 'A'
   or his 'Catullus', and
      recalling how I met him
once, reluctantly though
   rewardingly in the event,
      and how he is dead, I am left
with the conjecture poets
   have treated me with as much
      compassionate gentleness as
we might ascribe to centaurs
   finding within their troop
      either a man or a horse.

When I consider these
   whose operations are
      not beyond me but
as it were beside me
   in an alternative cosmos
      I do not envy them.

*Immortal Longings.*
*Before Surgery*

So now we know the worst.
    We start to count it up
    And it is not so bad;
We have an almighty thirst,
    As always, for a cup
    That is not to be had.

And this is nothing new.
    Such croaking throats as we
    Communed with, even at best!
The thirst – me wanting you,
    You half-possessing me –
    Always distracted, vexed...

Whoever it was that thought
    We needed scaring, erred.
    Whichever first must die,
The one and the other throat
    Will always answer a word
    Together: 'Dry...I'm *dry.'*

For this is almighty thirst.
    This is the all-availing
    Unsatisfied demand.
We always knew the worst,
    And always this unfailing
    Remedy was at hand.

## Tiger at the Movie-Show

I was never impressed, when they presented
'Culture' as a mesh of learned letters,
Weaving a basket for Europe, to keep together fragments
Against a future dawn. Of course, from time to time,
After 'Mädchen in Uniform', after
'Marie-Louise' (to take a couple of films),
I felt what the beaky poet had implied
With his broken columns, and the pigeons pecking
And the rough basket, piled on a cart
With the parrot and the family bible, when the bombers come.

At bottom it will all become a question
Of procédé, of talent and tradition, of the sense
Of 'saying', meaning an event, in the first place
And secondly what is said. And very often
We don't consider the created thing
But the ceremonies of creation.

For instance this 'Mädchen', this admirable film
Should pad about the precincts of my soul
A dangerous animal, answering no law
But those of its constitution, and appearing
With a shocking pertinence, on quite another trail
From where I marked it last. Instead
Two hours of the tiger's playing have become
Stuffed to a cypher, packed to a point to
Stand for something other than itself.
The difference is between the carnivore and the carved,
        snarling from thickets
Or else on a pedestal, yawning.

The singing robe of Europe is shrugged on
By every would-be poet. Some are weighed and stifled.
More seem ridiculous, and a few
Are dignified. Which has, as a spectacle,
Its own impressiveness, but which is never,
Properly speaking, Art.

To say you will stand by Art, with no farrago
Of decadence, and no wish to be clever
Or a superior person, means an intention
To outface the tiger, never to make him decorous
In stone or silk.

As for the pieces of Europe, caught up in a basket,
The thousands of Europe are starving, and ask for
Just what is left of the fishes
And a few small loaves. They will not pause to examine
The wickerwork of the roundsman and Redeemer.

## Fatherhood

Though love is the word a mother
Has earned the monopoly of,
A man with a twenty-year-old
Son has the right to say
In a grandmother's idiom, harshly:
'All children grow away.'

For a child grown is a child lost;
Grown up is grown away.
'Christopher Waddams is dying,'
You wrote to me today.
He was a bird-like bachelor,
Fellow of my college.

A sad thing, dying childless.
And yet a father of three,
Though the three have kept in touch
And given him cause for pride,
Dies as alone as ever
A Cambridge bachelor died.

## Reticence

Provided for! Provided for,
All of it, the horns
Drawn in, the drinking habits
Perfected, years ago;
In the expensive dawns,
The afterpleasure of
With difficulty rising and
Over his toast to know
This was provided for!

His devious compensations
Paying off, his pride
Force-fed to make the gross
Savouries of his silence;
Provisions made and made
Over the years, he comes
Into his own with an iron
Regimen over his drams:
Anger, malice, and tears.

# Seven Melodramas

# After a Change of Régime

A DRAMA IN THREE ACTS & FOR THREE VOICES

*for Don Stanford*

*Synopsis:* The time is c.1953. The Head of State has been manipulated by conspirators, headed by the Count, a war-hero; when the time comes, the conspirators require of the Head of State, suicide 'for the cause'. By the succeeding *régime*, Count and Head of State are alike found 'enemies of the state'. But the son of the Count and Countess, a lyrical poet, becomes a principal apologist for the new *régime*, and is applauded accordingly. The Minister for Culture observes all this sardonically, but is not adroit enough to conceal his contempt. The context is one Cold War; but the pattern persists through many.

There is also, sketched in, a *whodunnit*, but that's the merest device.

I

From the Widow of the Head of State
The Countess Remembers
Soliloquy of the Minister for Culture

II

Frankness of the Minister for Culture
The Countess Gives an Interview
From the Widow of the Head of State

III

The Countess Points a Finger
The Minister Disgraced
The Widow of the Head of State, as Ready Reckoner

# I

FROM THE WIDOW OF THE HEAD OF STATE

He was never above the mêlée
Of four bare legs in bed.
But what did the Countess say,
The groomed black head
Over the military typewriter?
I had gone there by mistake.
I saw her lips go tighter
And her hands pause, then take
A cigarette from her case.
Did she seek manhood
In the assassin's face
Of her own man of blood,
The mutilated colonel with the bomb,
As I did in the bed
Of one whose time would come
To be his figurehead?

I ought to have found it more
Difficult to forgive
The rôle they cast us for:
Removed, contemplative,
Statesmanlike. We paid
The heavier price, all told.
For Heinrich was afraid.
'Will no one help the old
Gentleman?' they said,
Meaning, to press the trigger
He held against his head.
Did he have to cut their figure?
A statesman has to fail
If the wife of a statesman needs
To judge her man by the scale
Of the crippled man of deeds.

They were planning it even then,
At the machine the Countess,
A network of hard-pushed men
And Heinrich. I counted for less

Than she did, less than I thought.
My contemplative man is dead
By violence, who taught
Civility instead.
Those professorial lips
He sealed against me earned
Honours and fellowships
Years ago. I had learned
From him, I had understood
How manhood is in the mind.
Then came this spilling of blood,
And manhood still to find.


THE COUNTESS REMEMBERS

I told him enigmatically: 'You need
Ventilation.' After a pause (he was
Famously imperturbable) he said:
'You mean, after all this, Canada?'
                                His wound
Had sobered him so far as not to attempt
The quizzical. 'Why, my dear,
Who'd rule it out? Kicking Horse Canyon for
Ever!'
        My limbless horseman
Had ruled out being amused, and yet amusement
Affectionately flickered in those tawny
Eyes that should have been Prussian. Easily he
Indulged me:
                'Yes, Saskatchewan. Why not?'

And yet he knew that, notable horseman though
He was on the sands of Pomerania, his
End had to be in the claustrophobic
Bunker, his bomb, asphyxiation by cordite.
No prairie airs for him.
                        Nor for me. And indeed I knew it.

Soft cats in public places ogled their cream
In the dish of him limping, laurelled by the *régime*.

'Where, where is justice, when the sacred gift,
When deathless justice comes not to reward
Perfervid love and utter self-denial...?'
(Pushkin, *Mozart & Salieri*)

Salieri to his Mozart – poisoner,
The sterile rival. If that Muse of his,
So bare and truthful, took it upon her
To know her peers, why here the parallel is,
Exact and banal. Calling him 'immature'
Gives me away; my lost youth makes the claim,
Wasted and Moscow-nipped. His never-worked-for,
Free, ambiguous mastery, all the same
I have the edge of – he should have a more
Responsible, a more adult concern.
He manages the thing with too much ease.
Expert in skills he never had to learn,
What can he see in them except caprice
Or self-indulgence? But there's more than this:
What Pushkin couldn't know, what this *flâneur*
Ought to know but doesn't, is
The right our guilt affords us. If I were
Free to tell this faithful party-member
All that the Party knows, were I to confess
The cost I know and choose not to remember,
I'd see his golden and unnatural youth
Age on the instant. And his truthfulness!
How cheap that comes, until one knows the truth...

Bored tonight, I took down Pushkin's trifle,
'Dubrovsky'. Does he know it? Poet's prose,
Bare narrative *résumé*, beautiful.
It made his much-praised spareness look verbose.
And yet I thought of him. Yes, reading through it,
I saw him cast just that cold classic light
On us, on the Revolution. If he knew it,
If only he knew... He can't be told outright.
But he's no fool. He ought to know me better
Than to interpret all my talk of 'conflict'
According to the letter.
I've tried to tell him, underneath the strict

Seal of our barbarous jargon, what the truth
Is, that he needs – not that he may tell it
(That he may not), but that its resonance
Tell for him. The elegance of the tacit
Informs the life we lead, and reticence
In art reflects it. Therefore all my planned
Exclusions should be seen as right
By a taste like his. Insufferably bland,
His blindness strips me. How unfair it is
That I, who know the truth, am bored tonight,
And he alert among complacencies!


## II

FRANKNESS OF THE MINISTER FOR CULTURE

'Know your enemy.' I know him,
Can whistle Dixie and
The Battle Hymn of the Republic.
I did not waste my time in Washington.

Because their kids are good kids, what their kids
Are avid for, they have to like as well;
Prompt action (swift compliance) has
Earned commendations. BCM (US):
Battle Communications
Maintenance. Crucial in Combat.

Or if their kids are bad kids by
Calvinist definition, what
Their kids have been inured to has to be
Endured by them for patriotic reasons,
For Uncle Sam's sweet sake. Complying, their
Abnegation gets to like the diet.

Parentage in America – there's a study!

AAA (triple A),
Atrocities Awareness
Agency: a boon to every age-group.
Of course it is their arts that are atrocious.

Americans live by acronyms.
And so I fear do we – a distasteful interim measure.
The measures ot verse must be that much more cherished and
     honoured.

Since we, not they, are the heirs
Of the Enlightenment, an enlightened
Fatherly concern for artists is
A high priority for the Revolution.

I should not need to spell this out, and would not
Except for the dolts among us. Turnip-heads!


THE COUNTESS GIVES AN INTERVIEW

Surviving was his business as a schoolboy
During those years of our sleazy triumphs, before
It came to be every one's business. Huge eyes under
The always thin thatch of his straight straw hair, he
Questioned: 'Was it not terrible?' I
Embraced him of course, said No, abstractedly;
Pleased by his sensitivity and yet
Uneasy with it, plagued by even then
In his piping treble the note of options kept
Open, and channels open, though of course
In the case of a mere child thinking so was absurd.

The mereness of him, of his or of any childhood
In those years and for people of our rank
Is hard to imagine. His father and I
Interacted so intensely ... pah,
Where did I learn such gibberish? Our love,
Mine and the Count's, could find no room for him.
And that's no crime. We found superior nurse-maids,
Then *mademoiselle*, then tutors. It was the pattern
In our world that was passing, not yet past.

40

He has favoured the public with precocious memoirs
In which – I have skimmed them – he accounts for
Father and Mother briefly indeed but with
Tenderness even one might say if one
Could so far trust him.
                              Yes, I am a tigress,
But not as you see in defence of her cub. I speak of
My son the poet who is having a great success;
On whose account you interview this non-person.

His patronage, or theirs who for now protect him,
Permits these indiscretions. You have been
Indulgent, comrades. You know better
Than I can do what character best projects him
Before a public that I have no truck with.


FROM THE WIDOW OF THE HEAD OF STATE

The English it was, he relied on.
A frail reed! Who was I
To tell him not to confide in
Their so amusingly drunken
Cultural attaché, their
Embassy spy?
                    I had little
To go on beyond what I heard
(One could hardly avoid it indeed): their
Journalists uproarious at the bar –
                    'Sister Wragg
                    will carry the flag...
                    Sister Barker
                    will be right-hand marker...'
(My English is good.) I heard them
Commending some one:
                    '...would as soon
                    miss Christmas or the Queen as
                    the glorious First of June.'
(The anniversary of a naval action,
Heinrich, I researched it.)

41

More I half-heard, wafted in and out
Of the Danubia's tea-time strings over cream-cakes,
The bar's increasingly loud and intemperate voices:
                    'The mind of Europe stops...'
                    'The ideologies rattle...'
                    'Nobody's easy touch,
                    Guy Burgess thought
                    Old England's winding-sheet
                    ought to have been sewn
                    by sailmakers and such...'

                              'Lest we forget!'

A ragged roar came. Then:
                    'One who sold as much
                    small dirt as he could get.'

The Danubia's tea-room emptied. There came through
one slurred discontinuous prattle:
                    'This is a common market,
                    trams continue to rattle.
                    This is the way the mind
                    of Europe stops, has stopped.'

                    'With a hey, jolly Jack, with a hey
                    and hearts of oak come home,'
        the voice said, then went dumb.

Heinrich, they spoke of one
Who had betrayed their secrets.
Leibchen, you should have known
Better. Perfidious English,
They trawled to catch only their own;
Their splotched own trout-farmed fish!

## III

### THE COUNTESS POINTS A FINGER

Who tipped them off about the bunker? Not
Istvan, not Karl . . . The field is appallingly narrow
Seeing that all who knew, who were in the network
Were rounded up and 'dealt with', there and then.
Quite in their style to kill their own informant,
That would be thorough. Istvan? Oskar? Karl?
Francois? . . . I would have let the question go
If it would let me. Some one said the leak
Could have been nearer home: the Count's *factotum*.
That loyal blockhead? Never! Nearer home
Even than that? That's paranoia speaking,
That must be chained and kenneled. Even so
I sniff our gate-posts
                        and come back with what
I cannot prove nor ever could: that drunken
English charmer whom I know my son
At times fell in with, in the Danubia bar.

Timid old Heinrich's Ganymede
A double agent? It's conceivable.


### THE MINISTER DISGRACED

Slowly destroying each other in transports
Of joy and rage the Count and Countess
Tolstoy lately stalked the stage.

Sheets were over the circle where children's
Voices would chant oh the song of the golden
Goose the principal boy of Panto,

And Claus or Nicholas all the grosser
Gods of the Christmas hissed the holy
Boyar and approved his Countess.

\*

43

At blood-warm Christmas booby Joseph
Feels a fool since pap and sleepy
Parturition seem the rule.

But I could wait. Their child the poet
Was mine, no other's. Children of my loins
Are not so dear; their several mothers know it.

Slowly destroying each other in torments
Of rage and appetite male and female
Mankind wrote the pre-war page,

Pre-Revolution. But paternity now
Is a considered, not a carnal matter;
Not once for all, but a perpetual Easter.

The spirit of Revolution easing
Out of that blasphemous egg, a mother's ardent
Good of coincident animal goes beg.

\*

I told his mother: It was not for me
To legislate for poetry, nor for her
Tainted by certain 'ill-advised connections'.

Some pride I took at the time in that
Civilized manoeuvre. Now the light
Leaks into my cell, accusing me over and over:

'Romanticized conception of the poet,
Hectic or pale *naif*!' He took a leaf
Out of my shrewd book, and impaled me on it.

I was the golden goose. This pantomime
Enacts the goose I was, and golden is
The price he has had for me, who dared to choose.

The time will come . . . It may, but I don't think so.
Thirty years on, he'll star in freedom-loving
Congresses where I'll be a dirty word.

As a researcher I'm no longer tireless;
Tenacious, though. It's not
The highest virtue, Heinrich let me know,
But has its usefulness. 'My little bloodhound,'
He called me once or twice, those years ago,
Smiling. I have my own techniques: I
Never let go,
And – here's a professional secret – I let chance
Work for me; meek short-lived gusts that blow
Crumples of information down the gutter
Bring what I could have slaved for years to know
And nowhere found. My swan's nest of grey hairs,
My reticule and sandwich, are well known
In the Academy of Sciences. I am not
Often saluted there, am seldom noticed,
A corpulent old biddy, but
I know my trade, and I am not afraid.

This time it was the merest air, not in
Metaphor but quite literally, blew
The crimped clue to me. It was the Tannoy
System one learns how not to listen to:
A bad mistake, a failing. Blaring from
Each tenement's or public building's corner
Came to us, day by day, what the *régime*
Thought proper for us. And this summer morning
It was, I perceived belatedly, a poem
Excited, high-flown, urgent. This was not
Anything new. For poetry too was the workers',
The ideology said, if they would only
Reach out and take it. And perhaps they did
For all I know; perhaps in the lonely *puszta*
Some herder of long-horned cattle half-remembered
What the Tannoy had blared as he scuffed his feet
Stumbling at dawn in his mired village. My
Allegedly muddier origins
In the small *bourgeoisie* had muddied me.
In our circles poetry was permitted,
Was even at time extolled: it fabricated
Idylls one might day-dream in. But this

Poetry made an idyll of our present
And thereby lied, it lied. I have been made
Indignant on this account – which will not do
For a researcher who should always be
Dispassionate, who very nearly this time,
Pulled by her passions, missed the straw in the wind.

The exalted diction, once and then again,
Swooped on to 'turnip-heads': not a locution
Altogether current yet, it seemed
(The poetry was ambiguous, as usual),
A slogan of class-division and resistance
In some one or other's mouth.
                                        For the researcher,
States like ours present a special problem:
Much that is said is said in code. Decoded,
This drop from aureate diction signalled, if
I may be excused the vulgarism, some one,
And some one of some eminence, 'for the chop'.

My cattle-herder on the *puszta*, what
Could he have made of it? It was not meant
For his decoding. The researcher knew
And knew right: fall of some one eminent.

Scholarship? No, hardly scholarship;
A matter of life and death. But it's on this –
What some one said, what some one else let slip,
The coral-insect's inching edifice –
That erudition grounds its hierarchies.

The obtuse researcher gets there after all
Or rather, first of all. The annalist
Sees in the tyrant's circle this one rise
And that one, who was more deserving, fall.

# A Heroine of the Academy

*President of the Academy*
*First Academician*
*Second Academician*
*Academician Fùrtseva*

PRESIDENT:
　　　　Elections to the Academy: referred from
　　　　Section Eleven – Madame Fùrtseva
　　　　Spokesperson – T. Afanasy Miliescu
　　　　Is nominated. I invite your comments.

FIRST ACADEMICIAN:
　　　　The Academy is a learned body. Where
　　　　Miliescu's learning is, we have been told:
　　　　In versions made from Pahlavi and Turkish.
　　　　Academician Fùrtseva's command of
　　　　These tongues I suspect is no more certain than mine,
　　　　But never mind. The case, we all know, rests on
　　　　Quite other grounds. The candidate in question
　　　　Is an idol of our youth, some sections of it
　　　　And those most bravely prominent in our late
　　　　Costly upheavals. It would do us good
　　　　Therefore to recruit him. Should we not, though,
　　　　Proceed on what we know? And what we know is
　　　　A ubiquitous bar-fly, clown, and womanizer,
　　　　Whose writings call for blood to run in the streets.

PRESIDENT:
　　　　That remark will not be minuted.

FIRST ACADEMICIAN:
　　　　I beg your pardon, Mr President.
　　　　Let me be impersonal, if I can:
　　　　We might as well elect the late Dictator
　　　　Who killed, who tortured, with such hardihood.
　　　　A writer's killings are all notional;
　　　　Does that absolve him?
　　　　Academician Fùrtseva thinks it does.
　　　　The Muse that she is or exalts, she exalts as exacting,
　　　　Extreme of its nature, not to be qualified.

47

Academicians, the atrocious Muse
(I grant she is atrocious) isn't what
We can or should be legislating for.

FÙRTSEVA:

Academies exist to succour eunuchs?
The cruelties of art we batten on,
Yet wash our hands of? That's despicable.

SECOND ACADEMICIAN:

Come, colleagues, let's remember who we are:
A faun and hamadryad in
Gardens of the receding Ottoman
Engendered us. And now we are to be
Severe of a sudden, so many impeccable Catos?
Danubian history doesn't permit us that,
Least of all now. We are ill-placed to open
Questions of art and art's morality.
All that we have to fudge, if we'd survive.

PRESIDENT:

Isn't that a little . . . cynical?

SECOND ACADEMICIAN:

No sir, it's merely prudent. For consider:
The emergent *régime* will not, any more
Than the fallen one, fail to secure
(If we are prudent) the Academy's
Fall-back position in
Public disturbances.
What more placatory, then,
Than for the Academy to designate
What drove despair on to our streets as
Acceptably 'problematic'?
We serve a purpose, colleagues;
Best we acknowledge that. Small price to pay,
Electing some innocuous demagogue.

PRESIDENT:

I will not put the question while such passions
Rage in the chamber, though we have other business.

48

FIRST ACADEMICIAN:

> 'Rage in the chamber...' Always chamber-music:
> The best we manage here is closet-drama.

SECOND ACADEMICIAN:

> And just as well. Drama out of the closet
> Means, we have all seen, corpses in the streets.
> All nationhood is mythical. Every nation
> Began, and in part persists as, a mere notion.
> Start from there, not where the myth says we
> Once were, but where we might be. Honoured friends,
> Between the February and October
> Revolutions a window opens.
> Look through it while it's there: this Miliescu,
> So widely loved, might be our Mayakovsky.

FIRST ACADEMICIAN:

> Perish the thought! Anyhow Mayakovsky,
> That demagogue, didn't have to deal with
> The *demos*, woman, whose emergence muddles
> All our already dangerously muddled
> Models of politics. Miliescu is
> Patently the women's candidate;
> On that score alone I'll vote against him,
> And if the bullets fly, so much the worse.

FÙRTSEVA:

> The bee in some bonnets
> Brave among bullets
> Seems more of a harpy
> Than my poor virago
> For all her exactions.
>
> Talk of the Muse is
> Gender-determined.
> A shame; since she flames with
> Equal injustice
> On women and men.
>
> Friends and dear brothers,
> All that we asked was
> (And was it so taxing?)

A straight, even-handed
Acceptance of bondage.

But everywhere, hatred;
Women mismated
Struggle for freedom
In un-free assemblies.
Ridiculous matrons
Playing Cassandra!

Hearing the hierarchs'
Tongue of the tribe
Clipped to encode the
Will of the elders,
What can they speak but
The programmed diatribe?

A harmless male person –
Voice of the many –
Is axed from contention
Because of a chorus
Of womankind's ringing,
Too fevered endoresement.

Fevers? We shake with
No fever that did not
Equally warm such
Heroes of freedom
As Rousseau or Burke.

Limed in the nets of
Partisan prudence,
Burke was a woman!
Singing a nation
Not his, nor in being.

Academicians!
Harridan songsters,
Birds of Burke's feather,
Crow over, bespatter
Your tacit procedures.

Rather than flatter
A paste-board consensus,
Here we abjure what
Token transvestite
Is foisted upon us.

I have heard colleagues
Debate Revolution
Through its two stages.
We would have fed it
Dry wood by bushels.

PRESIDENT:

T.A. Miliescu then
No longer has supporters.

## Bella & Rosa

### & AN OLD LADY

*for Harriet Wanklyn, author of*
The Eastern Marchlands of Europe

*OLD LADY:*

Voices, such voices ... They assail me now;
No, not assail, assuage. Did I ever hear Admiral Horthy,
King Carol? Oh I think not. And not theirs
Voices to oil my wheel-chair. Leave aside
Dear dead Stanley's that is with me always,
The voices that float in and out are *most*
Unexpected: one just now a station-master's
In I think Debreczen – such
A courteous man, in 1931
Or 1932, it must have been. And then,
Just as surprisingly, a choked-up voice
From a reception in say Nottingham,
Somewhere like that. Now why
Should that voice come? It had no foreign accent
Although the name was Portuguese, I'm sure;
Naturalized for centuries, it could be.
Anglicist in fact, with a solid
Reputation, Stanley said he'd heard.
He asked, with emphasis and urgency
Under the bland convention of those times:
'What are the poets of Poland up to?' Now
How should I know? Poetry was not
My interest nor my business, then or now;
Was happier with my station-master. Still
The urgency, it must be, brings it home
Across this tonic Northern air I can
Profit from for thirty-minute spells.
Now I am drifting off again. So good,
Those times, so good ... Tonic. I'm drifting off ...

*BELLA:*

Unhappy Daddy, drifting off
In an alcoholic haze we knew about
And wouldn't acknowledge. He was still
For all of that a clean old man, to the end.

ROSA:

It was that stupid poetry did it to him.
Once his delight, said Mother. I don't believe it.

OLD LADY:

Budapest no by-line; Prague was not
'The most beautiful city in Europe'.
I hadn't seen them all. And then, who has?
Such loose hyperbole! Poetical!
The press today is all such poetry.
That Portuguese-ish man, so keen on it,
Can he have been a reputable scholar?
Stanley knew as little of that as I did,
Hardbitten scholar but not hard,
Oh no not hard at all. Hyperbole is.
Could it be said that I hate poetry?
Old, a woman has no time for hatred,
No energy for it; young, I loved
Geography and history. Dear dead days
Of amateur and solitary travel
To and beyond the Iron Gate of the Danube...
A vanished world, the world the poorer for it.

BELLA:

Rosa, that new old lady in
The Garden Wing, she saw my name
Pinned to my shirt and she said,
Smiling: 'Portuguese.' I said
No, it was originally Spanish.

ROSA:

You were wrong there. Daddy when he was jolly
Would – don't you remember? – call us *portingales*,
What Shakespeare would have called us.

BELLA:

If you say so. Point is: she met Daddy
Or thinks she did. Do you believe she could have?

ROSA:

What does it matter? I suppose she could have,
Being in English or some sort of Slavist.
All of them live in the past, as Daddy could have.

BELLA:
> Why must you think so bitterly of Daddy?
> I don't reproach you, but it makes me sad.

ROSA:
> 'I don't reproach you, but it makes me sad.'
> Bella, do you want another quarrel?
> Our father had no right to be unhappy
> But was, and the blight of it has hurt us both.

OLD LADY:
> Learning the languages... well, of course one couldn't.
> A few stock phrases, for politeness' sake.
> Mostly one's English, failing that one's French
> Served. (No, that's wrong – the *lingua franca*, German:
> Significant I shouldn't want to think so.)
> Surprisingly often, in obscure small places
> The Hotel Bristol, named
> For a peripatetic Bishop, there before Thomas Cook.
> 'Cocooned', the so-called scholars of today
> Have said of me: cocooned in privilege,
> Milady, if you please. The funds that sent me
> Were ironmasters' dividends. And bright eyes,
> An eager heart, a scholarly conscience – my
> Sirs, the young forager had flown, for all
> Your one more heedless metaphor.
> > Baroque
> Small country towns, tiled roofs and cobbled streets,
> Storks in their season everywhere, on belfries
> With onion cupolas. Still bringing babies?
> Are there storks still in the – wait a minute –
> The *Alföld*? I am glad to think so, yes.

ROSA:
> Bad enough, the queer outlandish name.
> But then having nothing to back it up with, in
> School, I mean. Portuguese – did he ever
> Teach us a word of it? Had he a word to teach?
> Too much like hard work!

BELLA:
> > It's true I sometimes

54

Dreamed of a castle in Leon, Aragon,
Coimbra, is it? Or at least a parchment's
Dubious claim to some such. I confess I
Sometimes said there was, to satisfy
You know, the young men.

ROSA:

The one satisfaction
They ever got from either of us, my dear!

BELLA:

Rosa, that affair of our not having
Married, or had the chance of it, is not
(Remember, dear) worth speaking about. At our age!

ROSA:

Yes, yes, I know. And whether it was his fault. But, Bella,
Remember his castles not in Spain but in
Bukovina, Bosnia, I don't know.
Not that we ever went there, nor did he,
Nor tried to. It was all –
Here we go again – poetical.
Damn poetry that has damned us
To being what we are, a pair of spinsters
Running a nursing-home for the decayed
Gentry of the islanded North of England.

BELLA:

Rosa, you've been drinking again though where
You find the money for it I don't know. However,
Never mind. He had a mind like that;
He dreaded things, dreaded them for himself
And Mother, and for us. Now mostly I
Forget about him, I don't thank
That new old thing in the Garden Wing for bringing
Him back in his oh yes clean, his upright, vaguely
Soldierly, saddening presence. Best forget him.

OLD LADY:

Nothing I'm more inured to: punctuating
My days by the recurrent, wearisome
'Soon I shall have to eat' (to 'force it down'),

55

Then sleep when I don't want to. Stanley dear,
You knew this under my bleared but eagle eye
Those last years. I pouted: 'You
Don't like my catering? I'll not cater for you.'
Bravely you pretended: 'Savoury'.
Hunger it must be, though it doesn't seem so,
Sharpens my memory: how the wagons tooled
Briskly behind the fair-haired (Can
Horses be blonde?) horses in *troika*, whipped
By tow-haired Slovaks, always Lutheran
There, in Hungary. That much I manage.
Here comes the clatter of the approaching tray;
And after that oblivion comes, as always.

BELLA:

The new one in the Garden Wing, she had
A visitor: fat, crumpled, but quite clean,
Polite too, one might even venture courtly;
Old of course but not so old as she is.
It left her quite unmanned – I don't mean that:
Quite in a tizzy. And he signed
Our Visitors' Book not with the usual scrawl
But bold and clear: such-or-such PAKULL
(I wrote it down), then unmistakably
'Yugoslavian Embassy', and yet
With an address in Harrogate! I tell you
After a fashion it quite made my day.
We're not so out of the swim, dear. Such queer capers!

OLD LADY:

I didn't like him, though it was
Exceptionally kind for him to come.
It was Pakull, who wrote (But who'll remember?)
'Réforme Agraire en Yougoslavie et
les Provinces de Bachka et de Srem.'
'The dreaded rock-sill of the Iron Gate',
He quoted at me, paused and smiled, and said:
Not any more. Of course I'd heard about it:
Downriver the barrage that made the great
River a pond (he brought it home to me),
One hundred and thirty miles unruffled pond
Drowning the underwater spikes, the tortuous narrows,

The races and of course the riparian homesteads.
And thus you see, he said to me, again
Quoting my words and smiling, though I thought
This time slyly, the Danubian nations
Attain at last to economic
Maturity.
          Yes, but the cost of it!
The downstream island, harbour of the marooned
Turks where, Apollonius Rhodius says,
The argonauts anchored on their return from Colchis
(Gold panned in the upper Carpathians to this day
Or to my day), drowned necessarily –
The ancient inbred Turks of course re-settled
'Humanely'. He was undeniably gracious,
Come, so he said (his English very good) to
'Pay his respects'. A vanished world indeed!
So vanished it might never have been, one might as
Well have dreamed it up and never gone there,
Declaring it to begin with as it were
Vanishable, adumbratable
(If there were such a word), a world
That, since it never was, can never vanish,
Invulnerable to time and change. Unhappy,
Yes but unhappy in the frame of things.
That's harder than hyperbole. 'Dreaded sill.'
Stanley, I will not think such things. I won't!
Still, dread all gone, what else incorporates us?

# Three Pastors in Berlin

*for Rosanna Warren*

NEMETH:

> I was the Nazis' padre, you might say;
> Magyar, you see, not Slav. Hungarians
> Served with the *wehrmacht*. Did you know that, padre?

COLLINS:

> I don't quite see what that...

NEMETH:

> Of course not. And quite right.
> Magyars were by courtesy Aryans,
> All that in the long ago, before you were born.
> 'His beauty to consume away like a moth',
> The psalmist says. But to the point: my claim.
> It is by right of, don't you say, *the cloth*?
> Pastor, I need a pastor; need him now!
> And not with a German name, for various reasons.
> I come to you. Confession and absolution
> By a protestant rite, from some one who's not German:
> That's what not I but one of my sometime flock is
> Parching for; drools for it, and from me won't do.
> You're chaplain to the Occupying Forces,
> And English too. Your chrism he'll think sterling.

COLLINS:

> Oh my Lord – I don't mean that, but oh
> Gosh! I'll be glad to oblige. It's rather
> Out of my line (which is dealing with kiddies, mostly),
> But I expect the drill is in the Prayer Book.
> As everything is, if you look. It calls for some
> Study though, and prayer. The penitent
> Is not, I suppose, available just now.
> Oh he is? Well, give me twenty minutes.
> The church is two doors up, by the football-field.
> Goodness me... But wait! you say he is
> Protestant, I think my Free Church colleague...
> There are sects, you know, that differ quite a lot...

NEMETH:
>Pastor, all he asks is to be forgiven.
>In twenty minutes he'll be primed for you.

>>>>>>>>*[Departs.]*

COLLINS:
>Primed for it... like a bomb. Oh Christopher,
>Thank God you're here. This is a weird one. Listen,
>It's some Hungarian comes for absolution.
>I thought they were all Arcees in any case.

THOMSON:
>No, that's wrong. Plenty of Lutherans and
>Calvinists too – I can't remember how.
>It's in the histories of the Reformation.
>Except you'll miss your jogging, what's the problem?

COLLINS:
>Chris! Just think what this chap might confess to,
>What I shall have to absolve him from. Oh Brother!
>Pray with me.

THOMSON:
>>>>What? Oh all right. But no talking.

*[Silence.]*

COLLINS:
>Thanks.

THOMSON:
>>>That's all right. But tell me, Dicky:
>What if you hear things you can't forgive?

COLLINS:
>There aren't such things.

THOMSON:
>>>>Well no, that's true, there aren't.
>Good luck, chum. Rather you than me, I tell you;
>But our lot's not empowered, as you know.

*[Interval]*

THOMSON:
Well, you look perky. How did it go, then? Oh
Seal of the confessional, I suppose?

COLLINS:
Yes, but I'll tell you one thing: he was not
Hungarian, he was English-speaking Russky.

THOMSON:
Russky? But that's incredible. Wait a minute.
Fought with the wrong mob, did he?

COLLINS:
                                        Very canny;
Something of that. But set your mind at ease:
He wasn't the butcher of Lôdz or Lidice
Or if he was, he didn't tell me. Mostly
Fornications, blasphemies, run of the mill;
And something more, that I can't tell you.

THOMSON:
                                        Dicky,
I have to admire you, could have been hearing confessions
All your pastoral life.

NEMETH:
                        Excuse me, sirs.

COLLINS:
Pastor, come in. Can I present my colleague:
The Reverend Christopher Thomson?

NEMETH:
                                    Ah, delighted!
Three pastors in one place, three hoodie-crows
(Your Scots might say) perched on one withered bough,
Or rather on one withered, two quite green.
PASTOR Thomson, I am pleased to meet you.
Nemeth's the name. Yes, I am Pastor Nemeth.

COLLINS:
I was just brewing up a cup of tea.
Won't you join us?

NEMETH:

> Why, that's very kind...
> And as for the hoodie-crows, you must forgive me:
> I spent some time in the Kingdom of Fife, you see.
> While we're about it, the title 'Pastor' is
> Dubious in my case, I must admit,
> Like most things else about me. Pastor Collins,
> I am most grateful to you. As for that
> Brave friend I brought, he has departed quite
> Over-joyed – I'll risk that, over-joyed.

*[Silence.]*

THOMSON:

> Pastor Nemeth, do you perhaps not owe us,
> Me and my colleague, a word of explanation?

NEMETH:

> You think so, do you? Let's see; after
> My years in the Kingdom of Fife (I passed for Polish),
> Back to Berlin. To men of my
> Generation (I could have fathered you,
> Not many of us left), Berlin's the place.
> 'Fought with the wrong mob. Can't go home again' –
> Epitaph here, unwritten, on many a grave-stone.
> For instance in your cemetery one
> South African Air Force grave-slab, the inscription
> In Afrikaans. You fancy that equation?

THOMSON:

> Not much. And Dicky and I are not so green.
> You push us hard.

COLLINS:

> I'll go and refresh the pot.

NEMETH:

> He's gone to alert the guard-room, I imagine.
> Very proper. Your security
> Was always lax, I should have been stopped at the gate.
> Your people know me, though: a small-scale nuisance.
> A few hours' inconvenience is all.

61

*THOMSON:*

    And what about that friend of yours whom Pastor
    Collins so much obliged?

*NEMETH:*

                      His being here
    Was out of order, obviously. However,
    He's even less of a threat: a man of honour
    Such as I wouldn't claim to be. And brave,
    I said he was brave. I'll offer you an instance:
    You've been through Checkpoint Charlie, I suppose?
    Yes. Well, it's harder for us twilight people.
    For him it was unconscionably risky.
    He went through, and came back. And you know why?
    He'd got it in his head he had a brother
    Interred in the Red Army mausoleum.
    You've seen it? It's impressive. Forty or
    Sixty times over, I.V. Stalin lauds
    The Russian dead. Not Pushkin even once?
    No, not once. Nor Lenin. He came back
    Appalled, distraught. Fought in the wrong mob, see?
    Him and his brother, both; no help for it.
    And, pastor, that's irreparable Berlin
    East and West: a happy Babylon
    For your young soldiers and their gravid wives.

*THOMSON:*

    In Babylon the pastoral office is
    Harder than in encircled Stalingrad.

*NEMETH:*

    Ah, very true. I seem to taunt you, pastor,
    Because you have the authority I once had.
    That I envy you, but not your mission;
    Just as, unlike the brave old friend I came with,
    I want confession, but not absolution.
    – Which I'm to get. A corporal's detail
    Is stamping underneath us, and high time.
    Pastor, goodbye. And thank you. It's not often
    I get to have some clerical conversation.
    'His beauty to consume away like a moth',
    You might remember; and remember me
    Possibly in your prayers from time to time?

# Chernobyl. A Disaster

for Thom Gunn

Chernobyl: a defecting author
Overculme: his English translator and at need interpreter
Dignitary
Interviewer
Assassin

AT THE AIRPORT

OVERCULME:

Mr Chernobyl is
Tired and despairing. Besides
As a classical poet, he is
In any case sparing of words.
He hopes you will understand.

INTERVIEWER:

Sir, while respecting Mr
Chernobyl's unwillingness
At this time to venture
Remarks of a political nature,
Could he favour us with his reaction
To the just announced award
Of the Nobel Prize for Literature
To an East European author?

CHERNOBYL:

Eh, what? What? Oh the so-called
Minimalist, it must be. (Stupid Czech!)
It is all of it costume-drama. Look, we are as good at
Turning things round and upside down
As any of you are. Having, you might say, fewer
Pieces in play we overturn the chessboard
Sooner than you do. We can better afford it.

A *genre*-painting: board gone sprawling
Over the dirt-floor in the dirty light,
Indigenous, you are meant to understand.
No Flemish draperies, viols, virginals; no!
Slick boards, bare crusts, and sticks of furniture...

63

OVERCULME:
> Mr Chernobyl says . . .

CHERNOBYL:
> I haven't finished.
> Every penurious nation has its one
> Accredited monument: the national bard,
> Crammed down the gullets of gymnasiasts
> Whatever the régime. To denigrate him
> By parody and impudent distortion
> Costs nothing, and goes down well, and is
> The merest child's play: coarsen
> His metres to begin with . . .

INTERVIEWER:
> I haven't understood him, not a word.

OVERCULME:
> Mr Chernobyl has not heard
> News of the award;
> When he does, he will be happy
> To speak of it for the record.

INTERVIEWER:
> Let us be the first to tell him:
> It is a Slovakian lady;
> Her name is hard to pronounce.

CHERNOBYL:
> What did he say?

OVERCULME:
> Oh nothing.
> It's some Slovakian tart. You guessed it wrong.
> Now get into the car.

CHERNOBYL:
> A woman!

OVERCULME:
> Mitya,
> Save it for now. Remember where you are.

# IN THE MINISTRY

*ASSASSIN:*

> He is, I submit, irrelevant: a one-off
> Disaster waiting to happen. History,
> Finding no earthly use for him, writes him off.
> Why should we help history along?

*DIGNITARY:*

> Daughter, I am in charge here – don't
> Assume too much. Still, I approve your gumption:
> Chernobyl, an ill-aimed missile, will
> Undoubtedly self-destruct. Why then destroy him?
> The answer, I fear, is metaphysical.
> And metaphysics wasn't in your training.

*ASSASSIN:*

> With all respect, economy in
> Means to ends, I was taught. And isn't that
> (I beg your pardon) metaphysical?

*DIGNITARY:*

> No, it is a principle of aesthetics,
> And though a key one, not I'm afraid conclusive.
> 'Say what you have to say, then stop':
> The rule rebukes the bureaucrat, but also
> Such as him, freewheeling into saying
> What he had not known he meant to say
> Until he said it. Therefore you mistake him,
> You and whoever sent you. Merioneth
> Sheep make tainted mutton for his sake
> And spruces brown in Norway. Do you think
> A pistol-shot eradicates his persistence,
> Maker of stanzas, rooms and cyclotrons?
>
> The God of Hosts, of all the hosts of creatures,
> Underwrites him, don't you see? And though you
> Wish, I perceive, that he be quarantined
> In a canton of 'Who cares?' (Who cares Derzhavin had
> Metres to fox the prosodist?), *I* care.
> And therefore, daughter, you will take the gun
> That will be slipped you after you pass the screening

And you will use it, as you have been taught to.
You give the signal; it's 'Slovakia'.


IN THE HALL OF DELEGATES

*DIGNITARY:*

    In the Alice-in-Wonderland language
    That I find on these occasions
    Inescapable, every one
    So far has won a prize.
    But let me remind the Congress: our remit
    (A grievous one, I'll be the first to admit)
    Is to make 'the classical'
    Propitious to modern eyes.

    Mr Chernobyl, would you care to lead us
    Into our second session...?

*OVERCULME:*

    It's all yours, Cherners. Now remember:
    Slovaks, you think, are renegade seceders
    From a Pan-Slav Federation. *But don't say so!*

*CHERNOBYL:*

    What I would say to you, our dear
    Colleagues from the liberated West,
    Is that our emptied larders pre-empt yours.
    Our ikons are up for sale as yours are not;
    Though yours are too. We have much less to lose.
    Our canon's so discredited we can
    Overturn it and make mock of it
    As you must sweat a little to unseat yours.

    Let me recount an anecdote: on my
    Transit here, some months ago, I stayed
    With a Berliner friend. One afternoon,
    Dodging the Press, my comrade-writer took me...
    To what a wonderland! My friends, what riches!
    Netherlandish, early German treasures...
    And shall I tell you what entranced me most?

The furniture! The Fleming couple, their
Uxoriousness, fastidiously severe,
Ought to have moved me; but I fell
In love instead with a downfall of green fabric
Behind their unbending backs. Conspicuous
Consumption. Vulgar. But a vulgar Russian
Conceives this as the classical: the costly.
(The sumptuous, not the expensive.)

Our pinched poor writings elevate the bare;
In this, you emulate us. But I ask
*Luxuria*: metre, assonance, orchestration.
Short of that rhetorical surplus nothing
But comes out mean. Crystal, majolica-ware,
Entablatures, and hyperbolical scroll-work –
All that I crave. I hunger for those bounties.

Frugality, you will say to me: a terse
Economy in fitting means to ends –
Nerve of the classical! My friends,
I have survived the labour-camps. The lice
Are not so frugal there, and not so nice:
Them we must emulate, if we would survive them.

ASSASSIN:
        I am a delegate, Mr Chairman. How
Can any of us here refuse
Mr Chernobyl's wrenching paradox?
Frugality is one felicity
Known only to the profuse.
The classic husbanding of means to ends
Means having first sufficient choice of means;
Infinite, ideally.
                I've a question
For Mr Chernobyl: who was ever,
Or is, the national poet of the Slovaks?

*Pause. Then a storm of gunfire. Yells. Screams. Turmoil.*

DIGNITARY *(breathless):*
        She got the signal wrong, the wretched girl.
Eight guns at least, where two would have done the trick.

As always, metaphysics turns out messy.
This could have been an elegant operation.
Instead the disaster walks, sedately frantic;
Chernobyl lives, to alarm another day.

# Balancing Acts

## A SMALL DRAMA IN THREE SCENES

*Seamus*
*Shelagh*
*Eamonn*

*Donovan*

## SCENE ONE

*SEAMUS:*

    *Traditore, traduttore* – spare us!
    Of course the harsh Italian makes good sense
    Though nothing but an easy rigmarole.
    Translator/ traitor, yes; but how if we
    Reversed the proposition? Treachery
    Would come to seem a civilised occupation,
    Facilitating traffic over frontiers,
    Bringing what's dark to light (by selling secrets).
    That's what my Granda did, translating us
    From Herzegovina to County Louth.
    (Not that he sold us; I've no cause to think so.)

*SHELAGH:*

    You with your Italian! I don't mind it.
    Is it that same old Gramshie?

*SEAMUS:*

                 Gramsci! Shelagh,
    You astonish me: you move around,
    Heeding my talk with half your mind at most
    And something lodges. No, love, it's not Gramsci.

*SHELAGH:*

    Just as well; he was a communist.

*SEAMUS:*

    Not in the sense you mean, but never mind.

*SHELAGH:*

    It's true I only give you half my mind,

There's chores to do. When you go muttering
Half to yourself and half to me, it's homely.
You're like a kettle simmering on the hob
And when you're boiling dry I have to wet you
With an ignorant question. So what's *Herze*...
*Herze* – whatever-it-is? It's news to me:
I thought your Da was Yugoslavian.

SEAMUS:

He was, we are; for all we are
True Irish, Irish-born, the three of us,
Me and Siobhan and Eamonn. Don't you see?
That shows what a translator Granda was.
(Not Da, he was but a schoolboy.) Not
A stitch or a snag in the one of us, to show
There was an original we're translated from.

SHELAGH:

That's great, I'm sure. But what about this *Herz*...
Isn't it Yugoslavia?

SEAMUS:

Yes, it is;
As Connacht's Ireland.

SHELAGH:

And as Ulster is.

SEAMUS:

Ah yes, very like indeed, or so I'm told.
There's Herzegovina and Bosnia,
Macedonia, Serbia, Montenegro,
Slovenia, Croatia... that enough?

SHELAGH:

More than enough. Ireland has only four
Provinces, and they can't fend together.

SEAMUS:

If you attend, I'll tell you something else:
Not all Mohammedans always had brown faces.
Bits, large bits, of Yugoslavia were

70

Hungarian, Austrian, Turkish. And the Turks
Were there the longest. Can't you see
How, like the potato Protestants in this country,
A Bosnian might see benefits in the mosque?
Apostasy! The acme of translation!

SHELAGH:
Ah get away with you! You want to scare me,
Mister Schoolmaster. You are as good
A Catholic as most people in this town,
Though your brother and sister are better, and despite you
Study atheists like your precious Gramshie
Who was (yes, I attend more than you think)
A traitor, wasn't he? Went to prison for it?
– Enough of nonsense! On the morrow you
Visit your Granda. You want sandwiches?

SEAMUS:
I do, but I . . . Shelagh, don't walk away!


SCENE TWO

EAMONN:
So, and you've seen the ould disgraceful fella
Lately, have you?

SEAMUS:
                    He's had visitors.

EAMONN:
Has he now? And much good it may do them.

SEAMUS:
Depends what good they looked for. I don't like it.
I visit him quite regular; you don't.
There in the Home he has perked up a bit
Thanks to the Sisters, talks quite lucidly
For minutes at a time. At least he seems to.
And that's what I don't like.

71

EAMONN:

He talks of us?

SEAMUS:

Not at all. Of long before we were thought of;
Of Niko this, of Slobodan
Such and such. He talks of partisans,
Chetniks and Ustachi, Klagenfurt...
What's weird is that he talks of them in English.
And there's the trouble: strangers at his bedside
Might get him wrong. He's very prompt with names,
At his best he'll even answer questions.

EAMONN:

What questions would those be? Who'd care at all
Digging up all that ancient fol-de-rol?
Doesn't he talk of Da?

SEAMUS:

Well now, he does;
And that's the worst of it. He said to me
That you and I by a mere miscarriage missed
The cyanide Da had for the six of us.
What six? Don't ask me. Last time I was there
He said to me: 'My son, your father was
Corrupt from the day he was conceived, too clever.'

EAMONN:

That's horrible, you could have prepared me for it.
Let me think... He's bad things on his conscience
That he won't own, but fathers on some one else?

SEAMUS:

Yes, on some one else, and that's our Da.
Cyanide ampoules – hard to find, I'd think,
In a Saxon gentleman's toilet-case when he,
Our youthful Granda, unbelievably lounged,
Austrian-Saxon in the height of fashion,
Through spas and gardens.

EAMONN:

Now you've lost me, brother.

72

SEAMUS:

It doesn't matter. Eamonn, don't you see?
He's fantasizing what an attentive stranger
Either won't see, or won't be prepared to see
Or hear, as fantasies. What that stranger gets
Is names, and some names maybe lately famous
Set to be blackmailed.

EAMONN:

Now *you* fantasize!
And yet not more than I have: you suspect,
As I have, that our dear old Granda (not
So dear at that, if the truth be known), he might be
What's known as a war-criminal?

SEAMUS:

He might be.
Younger ones, or untimely dead like Da,
Might suffer for that still, although he won't.
Who talked to him? By what authority?

EAMONN:

Leave that to me; I think I can arrange it.
I have some influence in this diocese.

SEAMUS:

Ay, and across the Border, I believe...
The harm is done. I had a call from Dublin:
I am to hold myself available
All this week for interview. And as for
Authority, what do you say to INTERPOL?
That scares me, Eamonn, as it should scare you
Though you've the Bishop there to call upon.


SCENE THREE

SEAMUS:

Mr Donovan, now the investigation
I gather is over, what was the point of it?

DONOVAN:

> God bless you, Mr Burkitt, none at all!
> You have, if I may say so, a distorted
> Notion of the police. We do not, as
> Policemen, judge of treachery, or treason
> Or (what's a more inclusive term) betrayal.
> We gather names, we work out circumstances;
> Our betters bury or else brandish them.

SEAMUS:

> A humble trade, so. Tell me, did my Granda
> Provide what you had looked for?

DONOVAN:

> Pretty well.

SEAMUS:

> You know he's senile! What construction can...?
> Well, I remember: it's your betters judge
> What weight, or none, to give his maunderings.
> *Are* they your betters?

DONOVAN:

> It's a way of speaking.

SEAMUS:

> A way of passing all the bucks upstairs!

DONOVAN:

> You need no lessons, Mister Schoolmaster,
> On passing bucks without the staircase creaking.

SEAMUS:

> What does that mean? You've investigated
> My classroom schedules, and my reading-lists?
> Interviewed my pupils and their parents?

DONOVAN:

> Of course we have. What do you think we are:
> *Ton-ton macoutes* or a Praetorian Guard?
> It's hard work, Mr Burkitt: drudgery.
> You think I care what homework you've prescribed
> These many years? And yet there's some one cares.

74

SEAMUS:
>A small obedient cog in the machine
>Of a police-state...

DONOVAN:
>                    Come now, that may serve
>The Lower Sixth, or Trinity College even;
>The stupidest *garda* knows the difference,
>And knows a clapped-out metaphor when he sees it.
>I don't serve a State, as the *garda* does.
>You can be assured no pupil nor
>Parent knows he's been interrogated.
>Some basic skills we have, enough for instance...

SHELAGH:
>Wait a minute! Here's Saint Francis,
>Him of Assisi, Hymn of the Creatures, done in
>Beautiful Irish by me husband. I'll
>Read it, I will.

SEAMUS:
>                    Ah Shelagh, Shelagh...

DONOVAN:
>                                        Mrs Burkitt?
>Donovan's my name, Pierce Donovan.
>I hoped I'd get to meet you, Mrs Burkitt.

SHELAGH:
>And now you have. I don't know what you're after.

DONOVAN:
>After, ma'am? Not after, but before:
>Beforehand, you might say. Whereas your husband,
>He's 'after', isn't he? That poem of his is
>*After* Saint Francis. And that's proper but
>Perilous, Mrs Burkitt. Seeing that your husband
>Has left the room to show that he's annoyed,
>I offer you, although I go beyond
>My brief in doing it, a word of warning:
>Those we would call war-criminals, by others
>Are thought war-heroes, worth the re-assembling;

And being a good Catholic means something
Different at the other end of Europe.
It all comes down to problems of translation,
Mrs Burkitt; and your learned husband
Is very well aware of that, I reckon.
You lose your balance, even thinking of it.
Prudent policemen don't learn languages.
Italian now, I'd have thought was a difficult language;
And yet my daughter tells me it comes easy.

# Another Old Bolshevik

*for Philip Edwards*

A MELODRAMA FOR THREE VOICES

DR P:

'Alamein to Zem-Zem' – have you read it?
Ah but forgive me! Always I
interrogate at first meeting. Such bad manners.
The book was under your arm, is not well known.
Myself I was a bookseller for a time.
You want to hear of that, I think? My daughter
told me: no more of all that stupid stuff
from years ago, but how it has been since –
'Reflections of a Fortunate Survivor'.
Start me off with a question...
                                        Oh,
that one: the office that I hold in
the government-in-exile. Deary me!
My office? It's a lowly one. After all I
collaborated, did I not, and at
a not inconspicuous level? One does not
live that down, not with the intransigents.
So I lick stamps, and sometimes lick their boots,
and am a lucky creature, always was.

My nation never was. You know the record,
our tiresome history: an imperial duchy
six hundred years before Versailles; and there,
to satisfy President Wilson, nationhood!
What a joke! Our representative
a coterie French poet, with a name
beyond reproach of quite the bluest blood in
the reedy reaches of the Pripet or the Dniester,
I can't remember which. And this was what
had earned one's – what's the charming word – one's *fealty*?

My dear young man, imagine it if you can!
I'm loyal to this gas-fire, this
malodorous bed-sitter in West Hampstead,
and to whatever pays the rent of it,
just about pays it, sometimes. Oh the farce,

77

you can't imagine. Do you know there is
a Wendish government-in-exile? Yes;
somewhere in Putney, sends out invitations
once a year. And what a stir of conscience
among the greasy sports-coats, when we meet to
draft our reply! Turns out there are, you see,
unsavoury squads at large in unlikely Sweden
blowing up travel-agencies. Of course
they are disowned, a tall frock-coated old
head of a non-state spreads his fluttering hands.
But how can we (such statesmen!) risk our good
relations with your tolerant H.M.G.,
your well-policed Great Britain? No, we think;
the Putney Wends must swallow their dismay!

You are surprised to find me so
jolly, you say. Well, it's a jolly business
don't you think? Now Mrs Mackay, my daughter,
who vouches for you . . . that's a jolly business
too: that I seem to have fathered
an excitable Gaelic Jacobite. She alarms,
you must have noticed, her compliant husband.

But now I have embarrassed you. Oh dear.
That Scotch you brought (so kind of you) it rather
went to my head, I'm so unused to it
nowadays, and at my age. Now when
you come again, I'll be as talkative
but more to the point perhaps, or more in earnest.

\*

LYUDMILA MACKAY:
Wendish? In Putney? Oh he pulled your leg,
how naughty he is! You'll get to know my father
but it takes time. He'll go to any lengths
not to appear embittered, which he is.
It's sad of course, but saves his dignity.

ALEX MACKAY:
Mackays were Hanoverian, he knows that;
it's just his mischief, making out he doesn't.

The history of our clan is very boring.
I don't mean that the way he would, I mean it.
Now, my wife's history – Polish – that's eventful,
full of pathos. Oh, not Polish, he'd
have you believe, but something more exotic?
If he says so, then it must be right.
And yet the name, you know for yourself, is Polish.
Lyudmila thinks the name Mackay has lodged her
in Fingal's Cave, to strains of Mendelssohn,
and why not? He and she alike
are more enraptured by a dripping wave
in Wester Ross than all its stupid natives.
Let the old gentleman have his fantasies.

*

DR P:

'The Captive Mind' . . . but there I go again,
the allusive bibliomane. I meant to say
the captive and the captivated mind
are not so different. Mendelssohn
enthralls some people, some are enslaved by Wagner.
The unenthralled, the unenslaved, who envies?
He ought to jostle with the cut-off jeans
and captivating maidens I encounter,
as doubtless you do, in the Underground.
Every one would be in thrall to something
given the chance, a chance that's free for all.
Who's in the Top Ten? It's of no account,
that's just the point. Oh that Enlightenment dream!
These are the unenthralled, who hoot and scream
for a tooled-up ensemble gone tomorrow.
They are not deceived; in fact, these are the free,
these are the hoped-for freedom-fighters of
here today and gone tomorrow. Freedom
in a consumer society is to be free of the market,
that's to say, enslaved by it, to be sure.
But what a painless, unperturbed enslavement!
I've come to love and envy it, such freedom.

No, I am not ironical. I am not,
as I did last time, making mock of you;

I mean it. I can see now what I meant by,
or should have meant by, the dictatorship
of the proletariat. Here you have it, in
glorious undiscriminating London.
And I aver, or rather I repeat,
I love it. It was what we laboured for,
killed for in fact. It was worth killing for?
Yes, and worth dying for, if Freedom is.

None of this of course must you report
back to my daughter and my son-in-law.
And yet why not? They'll only put it down
to the old gentleman – so they speak of me –
finding his feet at last. And they are right.

*

DR P:

I am Lithuanian on my mother's side,
does that content you? I confess I do not
care to be quizzed about my ancestry,
however deprecatingly. You
want to know what it was like, though you pretend
not to. Well. Very well, I will try to tell you:

The village wife, the greying civil servant,
the crazy gutters and the nervous birds
cried out for him: Mamai,
the little man with the enormous gun
in the hideous cap. Mamai!
Wind out of Asia with a horde of horses,
once the magnificent, now from a peeling pent-house
toting a sudden gun.
                        And in the stallion
seamen's pea-jacketed patrol
ranging, the sudden angels
of every Revolution, the wild horses
tethered to every lamp-post, and stampeded
by a little spur.
                        And you, you too have seen them,
obsequious querist that I dally with:
the liquid eyes, the trembling

80

flanks, the saliva docile
after the ritual clap-trap or a casual
pass of the hands.    It is always Fingal's Cave
for them in the West, but for us who have known the Tartar –
Lithuanian, White Russian, what's the odds? –
it is the gong of Asia, wizard-god,
Mamai the Great. The fragrance brims
the latticed alleyways,
a sherbet spiked with Terrors.

Now do you see? Of course not. Why I should,
my dear young fellow, burden you with my
specially cherished nightmares, I do not
well understand. It must be, that I like you.

*

*ALEX MACKAY:*
Finding his feet? He found them long ago,
you ask Lyudmila. It's his tragedy,
if that's the word, to have found the spectacle
of human doings, here or anywhere else,
a puppet-show of Folly.
How with that background – there are documents
from his pre-war youth as a would-be *avant-gardiste*
(in print, I assure you: poems, even a play)...
how he became a Revolutionary, now
that's the absorbing question. Mr
Ashraf, you study politics, I think;
in my way, so do I. But isn't it
remarkable, and falls within our field,
how many revolutionaries started –
Hitler's the obvious case – as failed
avant-garde artists? It's the 'failed'
that commentators fasten on. But with my
father-in-law as instance, it's the
'avant-garde', the varieties of it,
I'd like to know more about. My wife can help you.

*LYUDMILA MACKAY:*
Poor Daddy! Far from finding his

always findable feet, it's being swept
off them, so firmly planted as they are,
he's always looked for. Odd that, as you tell me,
he's never fixed upon your being Asian,
Asian (not ancient!) Briton. In the past,
Asia it was he looked to, to redress
his European rationality. If he's
stopped dreaming of that – and you assure me he has –
I'm glad of it, yet sorry for him, a little.

\*

DR P:

Our friends the Wends have hit the headlines,
Mr Ashraf! You have seen the papers?
Kurds and Croats are the touted suspects
for the atrocity in Gothenburg
but you and I know better: hail the Wends
though in a splinter-group... And we know who
the Wends are, don't we, my Iranian friend?
I drink (he'd disapprove) to the Ayatollah.
Desert ascetics purge the bloat of the West –
of rationality? No! Of bloat and blood.
Tell your masters I am at their service.